TIME
FOR KIDS

ACTION!

MAKING MOVIES

D1623000

SCENE | TAKE | ROLL

DATE | SOUND

PROD. CO.

AUTHOR | **Sarah Garza**

CAMERAMAN

032707

CINEMA TICKET

ADMIT ONE

032700

Consultants

Timothy Rasinski, Ph.D.
Kent State University

Lori Oczkus
Literacy Consultant

David K. Lovegren
Producer

Based on writing from
TIME For Kids. *TIME For Kids* and the *TIME For Kids* logo are registered trademarks of TIME Inc. Used under license.

Publishing Credits

Dona Herweck Rice, *Editor-in-Chief*
Lee Aucoin, *Creative Director*
Jamey Acosta, *Senior Editor*
Heidi Fiedler, *Editor*
Lexa Hoang, *Designer*
Stephanie Reid, *Photo Editor*
Rane Anderson, *Contributing Author*
Rachelle Cracchiolo, *M.S.Ed., Publisher*

Teacher Created Materials

5301 Oceanus Drive
Huntington Beach, CA 92649-1030
http://www.tcmpub.com
ISBN 978-1-4333-4949-2

Table of Contents

Movie Magic

The lights are dim. The theater grows quiet. The audience can't wait for the opening scene. If you have ever walked out of a movie theater laughing, crying, or feeling excited, you have experienced movie magic. A film may only run for 90 minutes. But it can take years to make. So grab a bag of popcorn and take a seat. It's time to find out how movie magic is made.

4

THINK LINK

- Why do people enjoy movies?
- How are movies made?
- Would you like to make movies?

What's the Ticket?

What movies are currently playing in a theater near you? There's probably at least a comedy, an action flick, and a couple dramas. If you look at the box office, which ones stand out to you right away? Some people enjoy seeing all kinds of movies. But many people have a favorite **genre**.

Action

Hand-to-hand combat. Car chases. Death-defying stunts. Action films have them all! The best action films include speed, suspense, and thrills. Danger awaits as the hero tries to save the day. These films get our hearts pumping.

Romance

In romance movies, the audience watches as two characters find true love. By the end of the movie, they have overcome the obstacles that kept them apart. A romantic movie could feature friends who fall in love. Or perhaps the characters come from families that are at war. Whatever the story, romantic films are famous for making people believe in love.

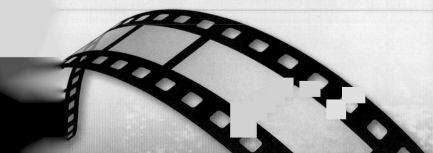

a scene from the classic Steven Spielberg film *Jurassic Park*

ZOOM LENS

28 - 95 min

DIRECTOR'S FAVORITES

Some **directors** are known for their work in one genre. Nora Ephron's romantic films are remembered fondly for their humor and smart look at love. For action-adventure movies, Steven Spielberg's films are popular with people around the world. *Jurassic Park*, *Jaws*, and *Indiana Jones* are a few of his hard-to-forget films.

7

Comedy

Comedy movies make us laugh out loud. Some use physical jokes. Others feature gross-out humor with lines that make you think, *I can't believe he just said that!* Comedy films stretch back to the silent-movie era and were some of the first films ever made.

Documentary

Many movies are about real events. **Documentaries** try to tell the truth about what happened. They often teach the viewer about a specific topic. They can cover everything from bacteria to galaxies. They may include a **voice-over**. Many documentaries include interviews with people talking about an event and telling their side of the story.

ZOOM LENS

28 - 95 mm

THE LOVE OF LAUGHTER

Moviegoers around the world love to laugh! In the last 15 years, comedies have made more money than any other genre.

Charlie Chaplin was an early Hollywood star, famous for his ability to make people laugh.

filming the documentary
Deep Sea 3-D

HOW MUCH ARE YOU WILLING TO PAY?

In 2010, the average cost of a movie ticket was $7.89. The average cost of a ticket has gone up $2.50 in the last decade. How much do you think tickets will cost 10 years from now?

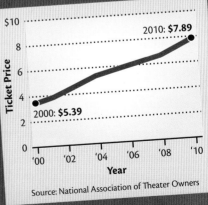

2010: **$7.89**

2000: **$5.39**

Ticket Price

$10

8

6

4

2

0

Year

'00 '02 '04 '06 '08 '10

Source: National Association of Theater Owners

Animated

Animated movies can be animated digitally or drawn by hand. They might tell a familiar story or a fantastic story never heard before. One of the very first animations was *Gertie the Dinosaur*, made in 1914 by Winsor McCay. This silent film was drawn in black and white. Today, animation features full-color characters from around the world in heartfelt adventures.

Drama

Dramas can be about loss, triumph, or a long journey. Actors often win awards for their performances in dramas because they must express intense emotions. People say dramas reflect real life. Unlike a romantic comedy, a drama may not have a happy ending. In fact, the hero of the story may even die.

MONEY MAKERS

These movies are some of the highest **grossing** children's films of all time. Many have made more money in the United States than most films for adults.

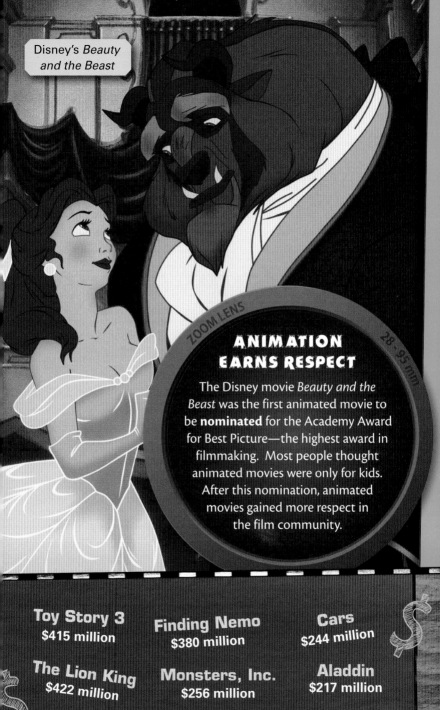

Disney's *Beauty and the Beast*

ZOOM LENS

28 - 95 mm

ANIMATION EARNS RESPECT

The Disney movie *Beauty and the Beast* was the first animated movie to be **nominated** for the Academy Award for Best Picture—the highest award in filmmaking. Most people thought animated movies were only for kids. After this nomination, animated movies gained more respect in the film community.

Toy Story 3
$415 million

Finding Nemo
$380 million

Cars
$244 million

The Lion King
$422 million

Monsters, Inc.
$256 million

Aladdin
$217 million

Horror

Hide your eyes and cover your ears! These are the movies that nightmares are made of. Whether they include aliens, monsters, or other strange creatures, these movies are designed to scare us. Early horror films included *Frankenstein* and *Dracula*. Today, horror films are scarier and more gruesome. Some horror movies appear so real that you might believe they are documentaries.

CHOCOLATE BLOOD

In the famous thriller *Psycho*, one of the scariest movies of all time, the director Alfred Hitchcock used chocolate syrup as fake blood. No one knew it was chocolate because the movie was shot in black and white. The texture of the syrup looked like blood to audiences watching the movie. This simple trick has scared audiences for decades!

Released in 1960, *Psycho* remains a classic with fans of horror.

A SPOOKY SET

Directors of horror movies want to scare audiences. Sometimes, they also want to scare their actors. Some directors do things to keep their actors on edge. They might tell the film crew to sneak up behind the actors and make loud noises so the actors jump. Directors want to capture a real look of fright on their faces.

Le Manoir du Diable, also known as *The Haunted Castle*, is a French film by Georges Méliès. This three-minute film is considered the first horror movie. Ironically, this film was supposed to amuse people, but it didn't. It scared them!

THE DIRECTOR'S CHOICE

You've received a call from the largest movie studio in Hollywood. They want *you* to direct their next film. First, you must choose from a stack of entertaining, well-written **screenplays**. Take the quiz below to discover what kind of movie you should make.

How would you like to spend a Friday night?
- **A.** preparing for a zombie attack
- **B.** listening to your favorite love songs
- **C.** training to be an astronaut
- **D.** helping a friend solve a problem

What do you love most about movies?
- **A.** blood and gore
- **B.** heartwarming moments
- **C.** car chases
- **D.** intense feelings

What moments do you hate most in movies?
- **A.** slow
- **B.** serious
- **C.** talking
- **D.** silly

You like a movie character who _____.

    A. can destroy a sea monster with a karate chop

    B. has witty comebacks

    C. can run fast, punch hard, and stop the bad guys

    D. can overcome the death of a loved one

It's night, and you are lost in a dark alleyway. You hear strange noises behind you. What do you do?

    A. Pull out your laser blaster and walk toward the noise.

    B. Quickly run down the alley, looking for a brave stranger who can help you.

    C. Step into the shadows, waiting to discover who or what is following you.

    D. Take out a weapon, and tell who or whatever it is to back off.

If you mostly answered **As**, try making a horror movie.

If you mostly answered **Bs,** have a laugh making a romantic comedy.

If you mostly answered **Cs**, get in gear with an action flick.

If you mostly answered **Ds**, be dramatic and make a drama.

3-D Movies

In a **3-D** film, it looks as if you can walk right into the movie. Objects appear to float in front of you as though they were close enough to touch. 3-D movies are shot using two cameras. Each camera records the same image from slightly different angles. This is similar to how your right eye sees things slightly differently than your left eye does. Both images are **projected** at the same time. In order to see the images in 3-D, you need to wear special glasses.

Scent of Mystery **producer** Mike Todd (left) and Smell-O-Vision inventor Hans Laube (right)

ZOOM LENS

28 - 95 mm

YUCK!

Movie studios have tried some strange things to get people excited about the movies. They even added scents to some movies! Perfumes were pumped into the theater during smelly scenes in the movie. But no one was happy about smelling the trash when the action on the screen moved into an alley.

3-D DOLLARS

In 2009, *Avatar* became the highest grossing 3-D film ever. It has made over $700 million since its release. Not only is it the highest grossing 3-D film but it is also the highest grossing film—*period*.

DIG DEEPER!

WORLD-CLASS CINEMA

Comedies and action films tend to be the most popular movies in America. Around the world, countries are developing their own styles of entertainment. Check out what's playing in these movie hot spots.

Hong Kong filmmakers are famous for martial-arts action films.

Films made in Bollywood, the Hollywood of India, are filled with singing, dancing, romance, and drama.

French films often take a thoughtful look at ordinary life.

Many Hollywood
blockbusters include
actors and directors
from Australia.
▼

American movies are
famous around the world
for their mind-boggling
special effects.
▼

Films made in
Argentina often have
small budgets but lots
of creativity
and personality.
▲

19

Movie Makers

Think of all the names that roll in the credits at the end of your favorite movie. Making a movie takes more than just the actors seen on screen. Movies can involve hundreds of other professionals.

Producer

A producer has a wide range of jobs that involve the business and production of movie making. An executive producer is in charge of securing money for the movie and hiring the director. A line producer makes sure filming moves smoothly. It is the producer's job to make sure everything from the screenplay to the opening night is handled properly.

Director

The director has the final say on the film's creative decisions. He or she decides what time of day scenes will be shot. The director works with the actors to develop the characters. The director decides where the scenes will take place. Directors work closely with the actors and the rest of the crew to make their artistic vision come to life. This is the person who calls "Action!" at the start of each scene.

Kathryn Bigelow

Director Michael Bay sets up a shot.

IN THE DIRECTOR'S CHAIR

In the 1800s, Alice Guy-Blache (right) was the first woman to direct a motion picture. She is also known as the first director of a fictional movie. In 2010, Kathryn Bigelow became the first woman to win an Academy Award for Best Directing.

Alice Guy-Blache

21

Director of Photography

The **director of photography (DP)** is also known as the **cinematographer**. DPs help create the look and style of the film. They need the right tools to achieve their vision. Choosing lenses, cameras, camera angles, and thinking about lighting are all part of the job.

Gaffer

It's the **gaffer's** job to bring the DP's vision to life. The gaffer is in charge of the lighting. The gaffer expertly chooses which lights to use to get the right effect. The lighting differs depending on whether the scene is indoors or outdoors. The lighting may change as the sun rises and sets as well. The gaffer chooses where to place equipment to get the perfect shot.

SETTING THE MOOD

Picture this: Two kids are about to go into a well-lit house. All the windows are open, and sunlight is pouring in. What do you think will happen after they go in? Now, picture this: With no lights on, the house has strange dark shadows, and the windows have heavy drapes to block out the sunlight. Do you think to yourself, *Nooo! Don't go in there!* Cinematographers know that differences in lighting can change your feeling about what is going to happen.

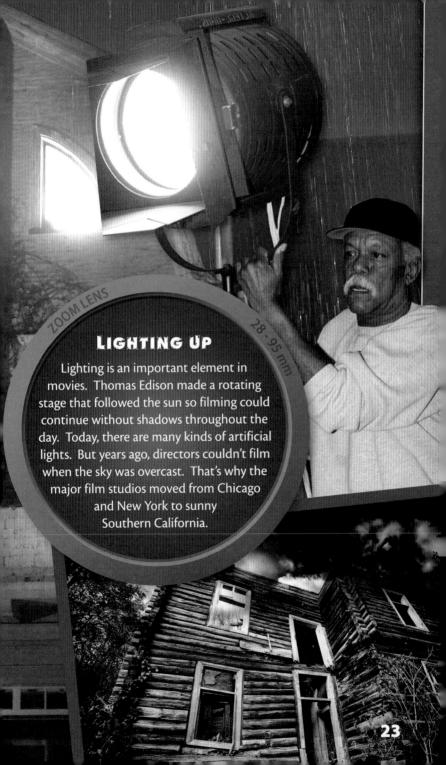

LIGHTING UP

Lighting is an important element in movies. Thomas Edison made a rotating stage that followed the sun so filming could continue without shadows throughout the day. Today, there are many kinds of artificial lights. But years ago, directors couldn't film when the sky was overcast. That's why the major film studios moved from Chicago and New York to sunny Southern California.

ZOOM LENS

28 - 95 mm

Costume Designer

A character in a movie about World War I is wearing a hoodie and jeans. Something is wrong with that picture. It's the costume designer's job to know what clothes fit the time period of a movie. Before filming starts, the designer sketches ideas and selects the fabrics. Colors may be chosen to show the characters' feelings in the film. The fabric and style must be right for the age of the character and for the character's personality. Some movies require just one or two simple costumes. Others, such as the epic *Gone with the Wind*, have thousands.

ZOOM LENS

28 - 95 mm

A HEAD ABOVE

With eight awards, costume designer Edith Head has won the most Oscars for costume design. Between 1949 and 1977, she was nominated 35 times!

Makeup Artist

The makeup artist uses makeup to help actors portray their roles. Costume makeup helps stars look their best under harsh lights. It can also make actors look tired. Scars, bruises, and bloody wounds can be painted with makeup. Makeup artists can even transform actors into monsters or aliens. Wigs, facial hair, and **prosthetic** facial features can work together to create an entirely new character.

A SCAR IS BORN!

During the filming of the Harry Potter movies, Harry's scar had to be re-created by makeup artists 5,800 times! Two thousand of those were on actor Daniel Radcliffe's head, while the other 3,800 were painted on the heads of his body doubles.

PRICEY SPIDER!

In the 2002 movie *Spiderman*, several different Spiderman costumes were created. Each of these costumes cost $100,000! Unfortunately, four of the costumes were stolen from the set and never returned.

Animators

If a movie is animated, artists draw each frame of the movie. Whether the animation is hand drawn or **digital**, animators create the world of the film and all the characters within it. Some animators focus on the characters' facial expressions. Others concentrate on the background and props.

ZOOM LENS

28 - 95 mm

FIELD TRIP

Animators often want their drawings to look real. They watch films or travel to real locations before drawing. For the film *Bambi*, fawns, skunks, and squirrels were kept in the Disney studio zoo. That made it easy for artists to pop over and watch what the animals did and how they moved.

Actors

Actors and actresses make movies come to life. They memorize all the lines in the **script** and act out the characters. When they are on set, they try to get into the minds of their characters. They must feel what the characters feel in each scene. Some actors are famous for playing the same type of character over and over. Others reinvent themselves for each movie so well it's impossible to recognize them.

GREAT ACTING

The best actors study the characters they play. They think hard about why the characters do what they do. If an actor can't feel the character's emotions, he or she will seem stiff and unnatural. A great actor can bring any character to life and make any story believable.

Behind the Scenes

Before filming starts, many steps must happen. **Preproduction** is a busy time. The actors are chosen. The costumes are made. The filming locations are selected. The production crew builds the sets. And the experts get the special effects ready to go. The director tries to prepare for any possible problems before filming begins. Everything is planned down to the last detail.

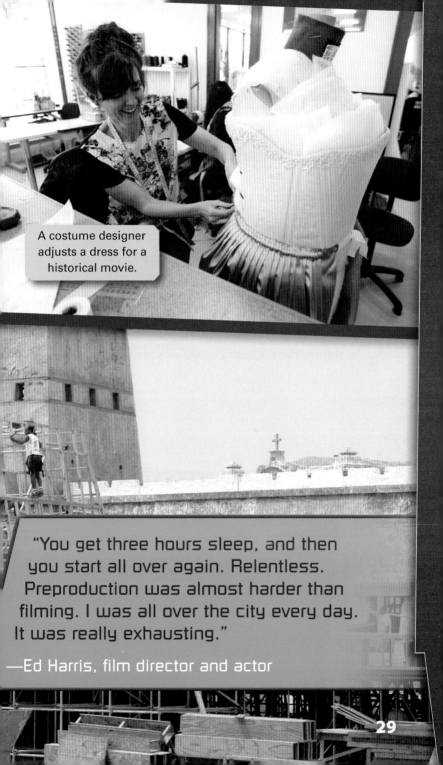

A costume designer adjusts a dress for a historical movie.

"You get three hours sleep, and then you start all over again. Relentless. Preproduction was almost harder than filming. I was all over the city every day. It was really exhausting."

—Ed Harris, film director and actor

Putting Pen to Paper

A screenplay can retell an old story, or it can tell an entirely new story. During filming, actors need to know what to say, where to stand, and how to act out their character's emotions. The screenplay tells them what's happening around them. Notes in the script help the director imagine how to film each scene.

Show Me the Money

Once the script is written, a production company must decide to fund the film. The production company pays for the crew, actors, and equipment. In return, the company receives a portion of the money the movie makes at the box office.

A FAMOUS PARTNERSHIP

The production company 20th Century Fox created movies such as *Avatar*, *Star Wars*, *Ice Age*, and *The Diary of a Wimpy Kid*. Originally, there were two companies, The Fox Film Corporation and 20th Century Pictures. In 1935, the Fox Film Corporation began to run out of money. So the two companies joined forces and became one of the most successful motion picture companies in the United States.

ZOOM LENS   28 - 95 mm

SCREEN WRITERS GUILD

In 1920, writers formed the Screen Writers Guild. The group works to make sure all writers get credit for the screenplays they write and sell.

In 1981, **screenwriters** banded together to protest unfair practices and payments.

THE WRITERS GUILD STRIKES

CRUNCHING NUMBERS

A feature film can cost hundreds of millions of dollars to produce. A **budget** is made ahead of time so the directors and producers know how much money they can spend on the actors, the crew, the music, and the special effects. The budget is extremely detailed and broken up into specific categories so every possible cost is accounted for.

A BUDGET MASTERPIECE

Item	Amount	Rate	Total
story rights	1	$1,200,000	$1,200,000
writers	3	$100,000	$300,000
script supplies (paper, photo copying, paper clips)	1	$2,500	$2,500
storyboard development	1	$4,000	$4,000
executive producer	1	$2,000,000	$2,000,000
director	1	$1,500,000	$1,500,000
actors	3	$1,000,000	$3,000,000

The horror film *The Village* had a budget of $71,682,975. But since it earned about $256,697,520 at the box office, who's complaining?

STOP! THINK...

- What is the total budget for this film?

- How is the total cost for each item calculated?

- In this budget, who or what is the largest expense?

Item	Amount	Rate	Total
stunt driver	1	$7,000	$7,000
set design	1	$10,000	$10,000
costumes	1	$90,000	$90,000
camera rentals	5	$2,000	$10,000
special effects	1	$1,000,000	$1,000,000
editing	1	$50,000	$50,000
		Total	**$4,167,000**

Choosing a Location

Movies may be filmed on location. But sometimes, the movie is shot on a movie set. The set could include a city or a house constructed by the set designers. Sometimes, the movie is shot where the script takes place. Other times, a different site may prove easier for filming, so London may stand in for New York. Or vice versa!

Filming on a constructed set makes it easier for directors to control the action as they shoot.

BACK IN BUSINESS

A backlot is a space behind a movie studio that contains several movie sets that can be used again and again. Building exteriors can be decorated to fit any time or place the director needs. Common sets include fake mountains, forests, ships, small towns, and city blocks.

Sets include just enough details to look real on film. Just try turning on the faucet in the kitchen sink of a movie set and you'll find where the movie magic ends.

Film Versus Digital

In the past, a long strip of film was fed through a movie camera to capture the action on a set. The film-strip was then fed into a projector that produced an image on a large screen. Today, we watch movies digitally on **high-definition** TVs, cell phones, laptops, and tablet computers. Likewise, most movies are shot using advanced digital cameras. Still, some filmmakers believe that shooting on film is better. They say it creates a warmer, more natural look to the movie.

PROTECTING THE PAST

Film is fragile. Movie studios take extreme measures to protect it. **Reels** of film are stored in caves deep underground. High-security vaults prevent thieves and natural disasters from destroying films. They're even built to withstand bombs.

THE NEW WAVE

Despite the love many professionals have for film, the industry is moving to digital. Here's why:

- Digital production may be less expensive.

- Film must be reloaded in the camera every 10 minutes. Digital movie files are saved on disks or hard drives.

- Digital equipment can be set up more quickly.

- Digital cameras fit in tighter spaces.

- Film requires more expertise. Digital cameras are easier for new directors to master.

- Digital equipment lets filmmakers check their progress and immediately see what has been captured on set.

DON'T FORGET!

The preproduction process is stressful for the movie crew! Once a script has been chosen, there's a lot to be done. The preproduction process is complex, and most things need to be done in a carefully planned order. Just imagine trying to film a movie without the costumes finished and ready for the actors!

1 Set a budget.

The budget lets you know how much money you can afford to spend and how many people you can afford to hire.

2 Make a production schedule.

Choose the dates for shooting the movie and editing the footage.

3 Hire your crew.

Some of the crew is hired based on their experience. Actors are hired not only because of their experience, but because the director thinks they are perfect for the part.

4 Visualize the movie.

A director needs to know what he or she expects the movie to look like before shooting begins. It can be costly to leave important decisions until the last minute.

5 Find locations.

The location of a movie sets the stage. Sometimes, the director will know the perfect place to film a scene, and other times, it takes weeks of searching for the perfect place.

6 Prepare costumes.

After the actors are chosen, the costumes can be tailored to fit their specific measurements.

7 Plan the lighting.

Some scenes can only be filmed in the morning, while others can only be filmed at night. Knowing the lighting needed for each scene helps directors schedule what time of day scenes need to be shot.

8 Plan each scene.

Although the location is already chosen, knowing the exact spot a scene needs to be filmed is important. Will it be at the top of the staircase or at the bottom? The smallest changes can have a huge impact on the way the audience sees the movie.

Lights! Camera! Action!

When filming begins, the crew arrives early to set up. The set must be built, the sound and recording equipment are placed, and all the lights must be positioned correctly. Sometimes, several scenes can be shot in one day. Other times, it can take many days to get one scene just right.

"I think cinema, movies, and magic have always been closely associated. The very earliest people who made film were magicians."

—Francis Ford Coppola, director

on the set of *The Chronicles of Narnia: The Lion, the Witch and the Wardrobe*

During the day, the crew checks the placement of props. They may adjust the sound and lighting equipment. Throughout the shooting, the makeup artists and costume designers are on hand to do **touch-ups**.

The director helps the actors in each scene by telling them how to move and discussing how each character feels. This helps the actors understand how to act during each scene.

When the filming is done, the crew stays to pack up. The actors get ready by preparing their lines for the next day, and the director reviews the film to make sure the scenes look right before they move on.

A makeup artist touches up actor Tom Hanks's makeup.

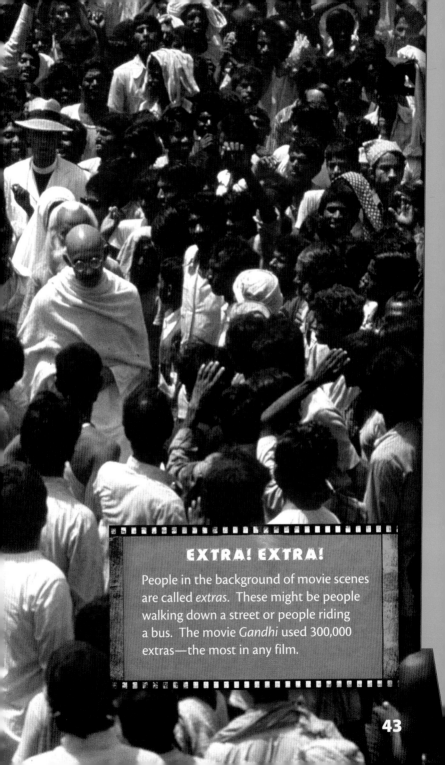

EXTRA! EXTRA!

People in the background of movie scenes are called *extras*. These might be people walking down a street or people riding a bus. The movie *Gandhi* used 300,000 extras—the most in any film.

DIG DEEPER!

TURNING NIGHT INTO DAY

The crew works long hours to get the perfect shot. Sometimes, they need natural light. But sometimes, they can get more footage if they stage the lights. Look at the pictures below to see how the gaffers create different times of day by playing with the angles and shadows.

If furniture, walls, or flooring are dark, more light will be needed.

Microphones are held high, out of the shot.

DIRECTOR

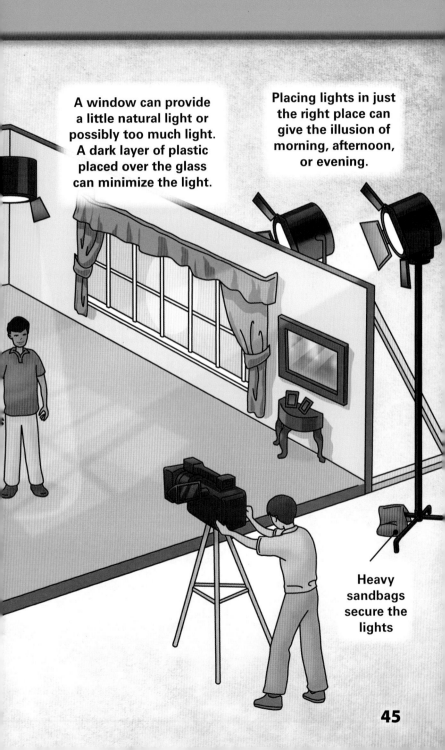

45

That's a Wrap!

The filming is finished. What happens next? Believe it or not, there is still a lot of work left. Things that are impossible in real life magically seem to become possible in films. After filming, special effects are added to the movie. They make impossible things a reality. One of the most popular special-effect techniques is **computer-generated imagery (CGI)**. Artists use CGI to make the terrifying fireballs, flying dragons, and deadly snowstorms that thrill audiences.

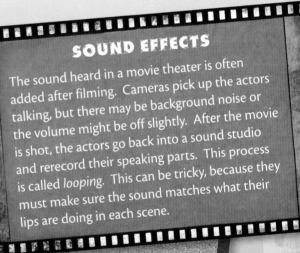

SOUND EFFECTS

The sound heard in a movie theater is often added after filming. Cameras pick up the actors talking, but there may be background noise or the volume might be off slightly. After the movie is shot, the actors go back into a sound studio and rerecord their speaking parts. This process is called *looping*. This can be tricky, because they must make sure the sound matches what their lips are doing in each scene.

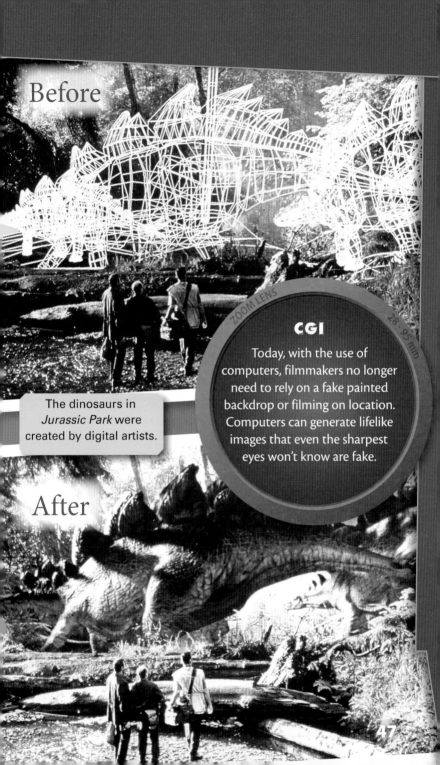

Before

CGI

Today, with the use of computers, filmmakers no longer need to rely on a fake painted backdrop or filming on location. Computers can generate lifelike images that even the sharpest eyes won't know are fake.

ZOOM LENS

28-95 mm

The dinosaurs in *Jurassic Park* were created by digital artists.

After

Editing

Movies can be anywhere from one to three hours long. But filmmakers usually shoot many more hours of film. They shoot every scene in the script from different angles and even some additional scenes just in case. After all the filming is done, the editor goes back through the film and chooses the scenes that best tell the story. Timing is everything in this job. The editor decides exactly how long each scene should run to keep the audience engaged.

Cue the Music

Think about the most emotional scene in your favorite movie. Now, imagine that scene without the music. Music helps the audience understand the emotions in each scene. The music can be light and cheery if the scene is funny or touching. Or it might be dark and threatening if the scene is dangerous or scary. The **composer** writes the music to match the scene.

Musicians gather around a microphone to record music as they watch a scene on TV.

"Film editing is now something almost everyone can do at a simple level and enjoy it, but to take it to a higher level requires the same dedication and persistence that any art form does."

—Walter Murch, film editor

DIG DEEPER!

SQUISH THIS AND POP THAT!

The next time you're watching a movie at home, press the mute button. Watching without the sound changes everything. Sure, you might be able to follow what's happening in the story by the looks on the actors' faces and the way they move. But without sound, you're missing an important part of the story. Sound in a movie isn't limited to the actors speaking. It includes background noises such as raindrops hitting the roof, the sound of trees blowing in the wind, or small things like the dropping of a pencil on the floor.

Try these sound effects to bring your next movie masterpiece to life!

A dog shaking itself dry?
Shake out a wet mop...
outside!

Elephants waving their ears?
Open and close umbrellas.

Horse hooves?
Clap two coconut halves together.

An arrow flying by?
Whip a bamboo stick past a microphone.

Coming Soon!

Most people love the **trailers** that play before the movie. They give a sneak peek at future movies. Trailers are designed to make you want to watch the movie in the theater. Ads such as movie posters or commercials try to draw you in. If someone is excited by the trailer or ad, they will tell their friends. Then, their friends will tell more friends. And pretty soon, the whole world is lining up for the midnight **premiere!**

ZOOM LENS

28 - 95 mm

TRAILING BEHIND

The first movie trailer appeared in 1913. For a while, trailers were shown at the end of the feature film. Because the audience usually left right after the film, the trailers soon appeared before the movie. But the name *trailer* stuck!

Movie studios hire teams with lots of experience to make trailers that are exciting to watch.

THE BEST OF THE BEST

Just as in movie making, there is also an art to making trailers. The trailer must show enough to grab your attention, but it can't show so much that it spoils the movie. Every year, The Golden Trailer awards honor the best movie trailers.

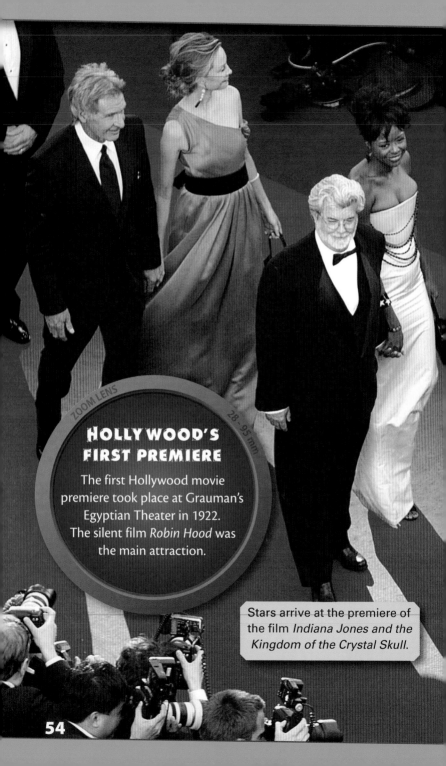

ZOOM LENS   28-95 mm

HOLLYWOOD'S FIRST PREMIERE

The first Hollywood movie premiere took place at Grauman's Egyptian Theater in 1922. The silent film *Robin Hood* was the main attraction.

Stars arrive at the premiere of the film *Indiana Jones and the Kingdom of the Crystal Skull.*

The Movie Premiere

The stars shine when a movie premieres! At the premiere, the actors, director, and producers walk the red carpet. The press interviews them about the film. They also get their pictures taken to **promote** the film. They want to encourage people to go out and see the movie.

Finally, the audience will get to see the movie. The long hours, money, and hard work pay off. Sometimes, people line up for hours to see the film. Some movies are in such high demand theaters schedule the first showing for midnight.

MIDNIGHT MADNESS!

In 2011, *Harry Potter and the Deathly Hallows Part 2* broke the record for the most money made at a midnight showing. The movie made $43,500,000 in one night!

Fans lined up to see *Harry Potter*.

Fin

  Great movies make you feel as though you are in the movie living the story alongside the characters. These are the movies that go on to earn Academy Awards. The next time you are watching a film, pay attention to the small details. Think of the crew behind the scenes, toiling away. And when the credits roll, silently thank each name for creating true movie magic.

Oscar statues

Have you seen the word *fin* appear at the end of some movies? *Fin* means "the end" in French.

The End

Glossary

3-D—giving the appearance of depth or varying distances, three-dimensional

budget—the amount of money that is assigned to a particular project

cinematographer—the person responsible for the look of a film

composer—a person who writes music

computer-generated imagery (CGI)—images that are created on a computer and placed into films to create special effects

digital—characterized by electronic and computerized technology

director of photography (DP)—another name for cinematographer, the person responsible for the look of a film

directors—the people responsible for all the artistic and technical aspects of making a film

documentaries—movies that provide facts or a story that is nonfiction

gaffer—the main electrician in a motion picture

genre—a category of movie (for example romance, comedy, horror, drama)

grossing—earning or bringing in money

high-definition—a digital system that has a sharper image and a wide-screen format

nominated—proposed for an honor

premiere—the first time a movie is shown in a theater

preproduction—the process prior to filming that includes planning and budgeting

producer—someone who supervises and controls the creation of a film

projected—caused to fall upon a surface such as a screen

promote—to attempt to sell by using advertisements

prosthetic—an artificial device used to re-create parts of a body

reels—an object that is used to hold and release film

screenplays—written forms of a movie that describes what the actors say and what the setting looks like

screenwriters—people who write scripts for movies

script—a screenplay prepared for film production

special effects—artificial visual or mechanical effects used to create the appearance of something that would be impossible or too costly or dangerous to actually do

touch-ups—to improve something by making small changes or additions

trailers—short clips of upcoming films designed to spark the audience's interest

voice-over—the voice of an unseen narrator speaking

Index

Bibliography

Kinney, Jeff. *The Wimpy Kid Movie Diary: How Greg Heffley Went Hollywood.* **Amulet Books, 2012.**

Join author and illustrator Jeff Kinney as his book is adapted into a live-action movie. From the first pencil drawing of Greg Heffley in Kinney's sketchbook to photographs, script pages, and costume designs, see how the *Diary of a Wimpy Kid* movie was made.

O'Brien, Lisa. *Lights, Camera, Action! Making Movies and TV from the Inside Out.* **Maple Tree Press Inc., 2007.**

Get an insider's look at the film and television industry, learning step by step how an idea makes it onto the screen. Test your showbiz knowledge with Popcorn Quizzes, get acting tips from the Director's Notes, and pick up industry lingo from Screen Speak glossaries.

Scholastic. *Harry Potter Handbook: Movie Magic.* **Scholastic Incorporated, 2011.**

Go behind the scenes on all eight *Harry Potter* movies. Meet the cast and crew of the Harry Potter films. Full-color photographs and interviews with the stars and filmmakers reveal how the magical world of Harry Potter made it from the pages of J.K. Rowling's popular book series to the big screen.

Wiese, Jim. *Movie Science: 40 Mind-Expanding, Reality-Bending, Starstruck Activities for Kids.* **John Wiley & Sons, 2001.**

Discover the science behind movie magic! Learn the basics of moviemaking, including props and makeup, special effects, and lighting. Then, impress your friends and family with your own special effects, using things you can find around the house!

More to Explore

Science of the Movies

http://science.discovery.com/tv/science-movies/science-movies.html

At this site, you can rate how real effects look to you and check out the top 10 special-effects sequences in movie history. Learn about the science behind special effects and movie makers' thoughts on the future of cinema.

Little Director

http://littledirector.com/index.html

Animate your drawings and make your own movie! Step-by-step videos show you how to draw, animate characters, add music to your movie, and more.

Mini Movie Makers

http://www.minimoviemakers.com

Discover tips and tricks to making movies, including how to avoid the top 10 video errors. You can join other young filmmakers in the Kid Vid Club and complete weekly movie-making challenges.

The Numbers

http://www.the-numbers.com/movies/records/#alltime

Check out all-time box office records in North America and worldwide. This site also keeps you up-to-date on weekly box-office numbers, and movie news as well as Academy Awards results and predictions.

About the Author

Sarah Garza grew up in Huntington Beach, California. She graduated from Cal Poly, San Luis Obispo with a bachelor's degree in history and a minor in English. She became a seventh-grade English and history teacher and currently teaches in Oakland, California. Sarah has always loved the movies, and it is a favorite family tradition to see them on the weekends. Her brother is making a career in the film industry. Sarah was thrilled to write a book about movies because watching them is one of her favorite hobbies!